# FOREWORD

Cars, lorries, trams, trains, buses and more are included in the pages of this little book, which I hope will a̶ ̶ ̶ ̶ ̶ ̶ ̶ ̶ ̶ ̶ ̶ ̶ ̶ ̶ ̶ ̶ ̶aps of schoolday summers when the sun always shone. In those days the various forms of transport around our ̶ ̶ ̶ ̶ ̶ ̶ ̶ ̶ ̶ ̶ ̶ ̶resting than now. Was it because steam came from the chimneys of the railway engines, and all motor vehicles haɑ ̶ ̶ ̶ ̶ ̶ ̶ ̶lividual to each type, thus appearing like so many friendly faces to the schoolboy enthusiast? Or was it because of the tramcars, ̶ ̶ ̶ ̶ ̶ ̶ ̶n't have any more, and for that reason alone prefer to recall as marvellous memories of 'the good old days'. Whatever the reason, we some̶ ̶ ̶ ys forget the downside. For instance, as a schoolboy in the 1950s who used to enjoy travelling on trams, I can distinctly remember the horrors of being trapped during rush hour on the top deck on a wet day. The dreadful and quite indescribable stench of a mixture of damp trench coats along with the searing smoke from Wills' Woodbine and Mitchell's Prize Crop still brings tears to my eyes, but not of nostalgia! Perhaps this book will help you conjure up some of your own recollections of 'Wheels Around Glasgow'.

Albion Motors built private cars as well as heavy lorries and buses until the First World War loomed, when all effort was placed on commercial vehicle production, much of it for the War Department. In August 1909, Glasgow Corporation purchased this 24-30 hp Albion for the official use of the Lord Provost. It was kept at the Corporation central motor garage in Dalhousie Street. This quote comes from a contemporary motoring newspaper: 'Glasgow Corporation have purchased a handsome Albion landaulette for use of the Lord Provost. For a number of years, Glasgow has always provided him with a carriage and pair of horses but for some time there has been a feeling that the time had come to replace this with the more up-to-date motor car, the choice falling on Albion.' The lucky Lord Provost is seen here with the new official car, registered G4, outside the City Chambers in George Square. He was Sir Archibald McInnes Shaw and was Provost from 1908 until 1911.

Standing room only as a busload of football supporters heads for Hampden in the 1890s. A paper destination bill in the middle window reads 'Football Match'. The three-horse bus was owned by the Glasgow Carriage Hiring Company, who enjoyed particularly good business on Sundays, conveying drouthy 'bona fide travellers' to various drinking destinations outside the city boundary where they could enjoy alcoholic refreshment and comply with the laws of the time. This picture, taken in Cathcart Road, Crosshill, demonstrates the popularity of venetian blinds even a century ago, since they are evident in every window of the tenement building in the background.

Until the advent of the first primitive motor vehicles towards the end of the nineteenth century, the horse was king of the road. This particular horse-drawn vehicle, which was owned by farmer Robert Munro of Polnoon, Eaglesham, and which made daily trips 'intae Glesca', became immortalised in the words of the old song, 'The Soor Milk Cairt'. The song (usually sung to the tune of the Irish air 'In the Garden Where the Praties Grow'), was composed by Glasgow barber Tom Johnstone, who regularly 'week ended' at Eaglesham, which was then a popular retreat for city folks who would often get a lift back to town early on a Monday morning with one of the soor milk (buttermilk) cairts, which left for Glasgow around 4.30 a.m. This turn of the century photograph shows the cart with regular driver Will Todd on milk delivery duties. Also pictured are the housekeeper, cook and two waitresses at Rouken Glen Mansion House which had a tea-room at the time. Will appears strangely oblivious to all his attractive female company.

At the turn of the century there were huge numbers of horse-drawn vehicles in the city pulling both goods and passenger conveyances, in addition to the many privately-owned carriages belonging to more affluent citizens. Naturally, coachbuilding firms thrived in this environment, and one such firm was Alan P. Blue of Pitt Street, who was in business until the 1960s. This horse-drawn van, built for Waddell's sausage works and butchery, is typical of his work in Victorian times. Vehicles such as these often displayed the best of a signwriter's art and the back of this one advertises Waddell's covered steak pies and covered fruit tarts.

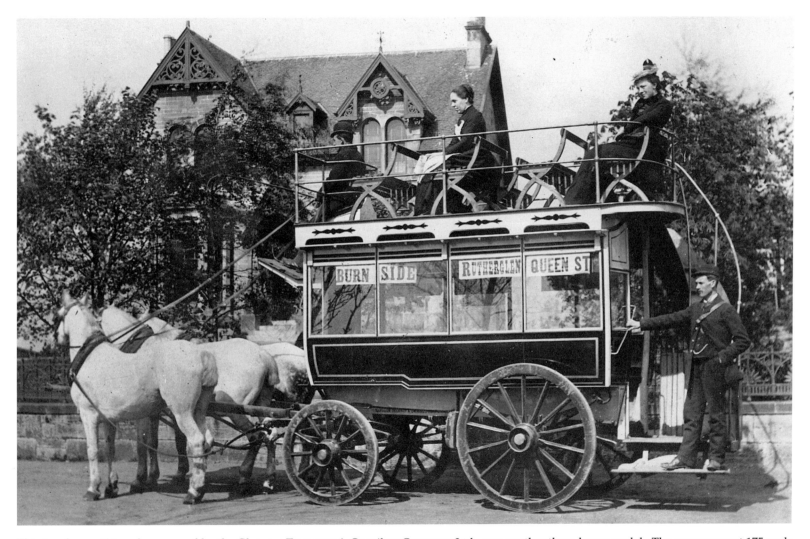

This 'garden seat' type bus, owned by the Glasgow Tramway & Omnibus Company Ltd., was another three-horse model. The company put 175 such 26-seater double deckers in service in 1894 to combat competition from the Glasgow Corporation horse trams. Drawn by three greys, this bus was photographed in the late 1890s in High Burnside at the terminus of the route from there, via Rutherglen, to Queen Street in the city centre.

One of the very first of the new-fangled 'horseless carriages' to be seen around Glasgow was this solid tyred Stirling/Daimler of 1896, photographed while on trial to the Scottish Co-operative Wholesale Society outside their Shieldhall works. John Stirling, a well-established Hamilton coachbuilder, saw the potential of the motor vehicle early on, and imported Daimler chassis from Germany on which he built this type of wagonette body. Early examples such as this had tiller steering, which was replaced by the more conventional wheel on later models. Thomas Morrison, at the tiller, was Stirling's first test driver/salesman but it was 'no sale' to the Co-op on this occasion. Their managers were apparently unimpressed by the vehicle, a fact that may be judged by their unsmiling faces.

Scotland's first important motor car trial was held at the Glasgow International Exhibition in Kelvingrove, 1901. Two of the competing automobiles are seen here at the new sports arena, which was constructed on the university athletics ground. No. 27 was a 5 hp French Decauville Voiturelle (a feminine Voiturette!) with tiller steering, which was the overall prize-winner at the event. The other car, no. 33, a two seat tri-car (note the precarious front position of the passenger!), was an English-built Century Tandem. Apparently this was the lightest and cheapest car on trial.

Many of the cars and commercial vehicles which ran on the streets of Glasgow were actually built there too. The best known motor manufacturers in the city in early Edwardian days were the three famous 'A's: Albion, Argyll and Arrol-Johnston, the latter known originally as the Mo-Car Syndicate. All three initially built both private cars and commercial vehicles, but whereas Albion ceased car production in 1913, the opposite was largely true of the others, who concentrated on their cars. Starting from humble beginnings in 1899, Albion Motors quickly gained a well-deserved reputation for solid reliability, necessitating a move from its original premises in Finnieston Street to a purpose-built factory in South Street in 1903, which was expanded as the business continued to grow. Glasgow Corporation naturally backed local industry, and this picture of GB 5317, a 24 hp van, was taken outside the main entrance to the Albion works in South Street, Scotstoun, prior to delivery to Glasgow Corporation Tramways Department in 1924. In 1999 Albion celebrates its centenary year, although now producing components only and not complete vehicles. The company is now owned by the American Axle & Manufacturing Co. of Detroit.

Albions operated all over the city in the shape of the many hundreds of ordinary lorries that worked hard for their living for all manner of owners. These examples belonged to Sawers Ltd. of Howard Street, who as well as being ice manufacturers owned Anderson's Fishmongers. This picture, taken in West Nile Street in 1934, shows US 5385, a new Albion model 41 with the well-known 'rising sun' radiator, and GA3014, an older 20 hp model dating from 1921. Nowadays these premises are occupied by The Nile pub.

The 1930 Road Traffic Act weighed heavily against the continuing economic viability of operating steam lorries in this country, but until then these leviathans of the road had been very popular with haulage contractors. The most popular make was the Sentinel, which was built in Shrewsbury from 1917 – although prior to that time the works had been in the Polmadie district of Glasgow. The builders were Alley and MacLellan Ltd. and this picture shows an original Polmadie-built product of 1907. Registered V513, this 6-tonner was one of several in the fleet of the Scottish Co-operative Wholesale Society, whose headquarters were in Morrison Street (although the transport department was in nearby Scotland Street). Sentinel claimed that the running costs of their steam wagons were little more than half those of a petrol lorry of similar capacity.

George Halley, another Glasgow commercial vehicle manufacturer, went into business building steam lorries. The company, which was initially called the Glasgow Motor Lorry Co., had a factory in Finnieston Street, but subsequently moved to Crownpoint Road, Bridgeton, where it began producing petrol-powered lorries. It was re-formed as Halley's Industrial Motors in 1906 when a further move was made to a purpose-built factory in Yoker. This picture shows a fully loaded Halley 20 hp charabanc on a pre-delivery test, climbing steep Gardner Street in Partick. The usual crowd of small children watch its progress with interest. It was registered SB 60, which suggests that it was destined for a customer in Argyllshire.

This horse-drawn cab was reputed to have been the last in regular service in the city. It was owned and driven by Andrew O'Brien of Coventry Drive, Dennistoun, and his horse 'Peggy' was generally stabled in the Parade Garage, Alexandra Parade. This picture appeared in the press at Glasgow Fair time in 1930 with the caption 'The old growler pressed into service to cope with the rush' – presumably referring to the cab and not Andrew O'Brien. The location is St Enoch Square with passengers and their luggage heading for St Enoch railway station. This station closed in 1966 and the present St Enoch shopping centre now covers the former railway site.

Some companies, notably brewers and dairies, retained horse-drawn transport up until the 1970s before finally submitting to the internal combustion engine. Probably the last horses to work commercially for their oats in the city area were those owned by Buchanan's Black and White Scotch Whisky Co. This 1978 scene is in Finnieston Street, where in an earlier era no less than four of Scotland's pioneer motor manufacturers (Albion, Halley, Kelvin, and Carlaw) had their works for a time. As more motorised delivery vehicles became available, the conversion from four legs to four wheels was of course hastened.

Among the many haulage contractors and general carriers to operate steam wagons around the city was Archibald Alexander of Fountainwell Road, Sighthill. (He had provided horse-drawn transport during the construction of the city cable subway in the 1890s.) These steam lorries were cheap to run in comparison to their petrol powered counterparts, and apparently cheaper still than a horse-drawn lorry. After a family disagreement, Archibald Alexander junior started out on his own, and by the 1920s was the owner of a fleet which included this solid tyred Sentinel steamer and trailer, based in a depot at 164 Pinkston Road (Doo's Loan).

This Albion of 1949, seen heading a line of lorries taking part in an early 1950s Glasgow students' charities day parade, was a later vehicle in Archd. Alexander's fleet. The parade was always a popular event and generated a lot of fun amongst second city citizens. I recall it always took place on a Saturday in January when Glasgow's weather was invariably at its worst. The students brightened the dark day, however, in their amusing and colourful costumes. They seemed to pop up everywhere, even appearing on board the Corporation tramcars, buses and underground to shake their collecting cans and sell copies of their less than squeaky clean magazine *Y'Gorra*, sections of which, by the standards of the day, were quite daring. The parade, which now seems to be a thing of the past, is seen here passing Kelvin Way at the west end of Sauchiehall Street, with Kelvingrove Art Gallery just visible through the mist in the background.

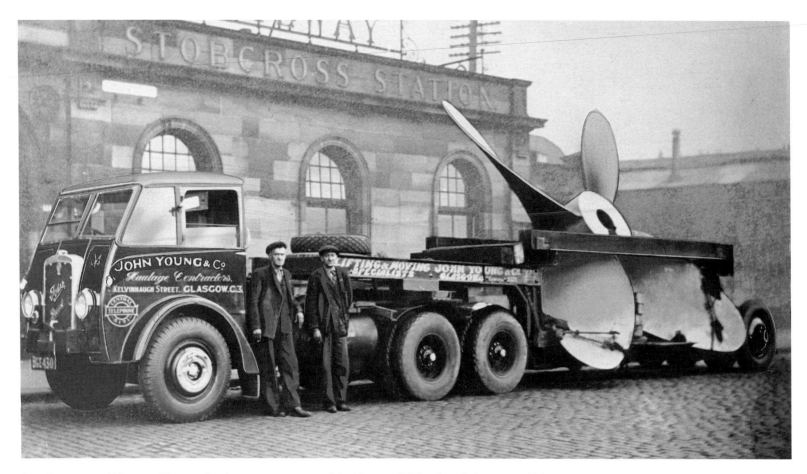

Another very well-known Glasgow haulage contractor was John Young of Kelvinhaugh Street. 'Bubbly' Young, as he was familiarly known (reputedly because he was aye greetin' an' moanin'), specialised in the haulage of abnormal loads, with the boast that nothing was too large to be transported, since the company could adapt their vehicles according to the scale of the job in question. BGE 430, a Foden tractor unit new in 1938, is seen in the late 1930s outside Stobcross Station hauling a ship's propeller. Because of its proportions, this required the construction of a special frame to support it at an angle which would minimise the load's width, without preventing passage beneath low bridges.

No matter how unlikely it may seem, this aeroplane was photographed being towed along St Vincent Street! G - ABDS, seen here with wings folded for safety, was the Blackburn Bluebird in which the Hon. Mrs Victor Bruce successfully completed a solo flight around the world in 1930. The plane was put on show at the Kelvin Hall during a celebratory tour around Britain in 1931. Towing it there prior to the event was an equally interesting vehicle – a Panhard car from the turn of the century with bodywork by John Stirling of Hamilton (see page 8). It was driven by owner John Bryce of Lanark who had entered (and won) the 'old crocks race' from London to Brighton with it in 1927 and 1928. This historic car was sold to a buyer in the USA in the mid-1930s.

A specially posed view outside the headquarters of the United Co-operative Baking Society Ltd. at 12 McNeil Street in the Hutchesontown area of the city. The pre-First World War delivery fleet of the UCBS consisted mainly of chain driven, solid tyred Halleys (built in Yoker) and Belhavens (built in Wishaw). Some of the latter make were assembled by the Co-op themselves and badged as Unitas vehicles. The Co-op also built most of the bodies in their own coachbuilding department. These ornately finished vans, complete with bread hampers on the roofs, were a tribute to the skill of the coachpainter.

St Enoch Square in the mid-1950s was really one big undisciplined parking lot. The stairs on the right led up to the balcony of St Enoch railway station (closed 1966) and hotel (demolished 1977). Among the wide assortment of private cars visible in this scene are various models of Rover, Vauxhall, Ford, Hillman, Austin, Morris and Humber. Austin FX3 taxicabs are prominent, as is a Guy 'Wolf' furniture van, while a Daimler Corporation bus leaves its stance for Croftfoot on service 5. All the coaches belonged to Lowland Motorways, whose head office was at the top of Buchanan Street, which is seen leading off to the north of the square. Some of their AECs, a Bedford and an Albion are in this picture outside the City Air Terminal, where passengers were able to check in for their flights before departing by coach to Renfrew or Prestwick airports.

Although primitive in appearance by today's standards, this fire engine was up-to-date in every respect when it was in regular daily use during the Edwardian period, and a vast improvement over the horse-drawn fire-fighting appliances which it replaced. It is believed to be a Panhard/Merryweather, delivered to the Glasgow Brigade around 1905 and licensed G 466 in the city. It is seen with its proud crew at Springburn fire station at the corner of Springburn and Keppochhill Roads.

Inside the Glasgow Central Fire Station in Ingram Street around 1915, with four of the then current fire engines visible. The two nearest the camera were Halley 75 hp machines and were built in Yoker, where Halley Street still exists as a reminder of this once important commercial vehicle manufacturer, who finally ceased trading in 1935. The other two were Dennis machines built by Dennis Bros. of Guildford, still a well-known name in the truck and bus field.

G 2301 was a Glasgow registered Renault of First World War vintage in the service of the St Andrew's Ambulance Association. The bodies on many of the association's vehicles were built by Cowieson of Charles Street, St Rollox. This same builder later constructed large numbers of both single and double deck buses for Glasgow Corporation, not to mention wooden sheds and prefab homes throughout Scotland.

US 5052 was a six-cylinder Austin 12 which entered the St Andrew's Ambulance Association fleet in 1934. It was bodied by Wm. Park & Sons of Kilbirnie Street, off Eglinton Street on Glasgow's south side. The registration letters 'US' were originally allocated to the Burgh of Govan before it became part of the City of Glasgow. Similarly, 'YS' was originally allocated to Partick.

Registered G325, this 30 hp two ton Lacre prison van was purchased by Glasgow Corporation in 1913. It had accommodation for 24 prisoners and 4 attendants.

In 1936 the City of Glasgow Police took delivery of YS 6887, an Albion H125 patrol van, otherwise known as a 'meat wagon', 'paddy wagon' or sundry other similar endearments. It is seen here when new outside a police box in the Knightswood area.

2 June 1953 was Coronation day for Queen Elizabeth and the British Railways locomotive sheds at Polmadie turned out former LMS class 8 Pacific no. 46220, named Coronation, in immaculate condition and complete with decorative crown to mark the occasion.  It worked the up Royal Scot, which left Glasgow Central at 1000 for London (Euston) and was photographed a few minutes later passing through Eglinton Street station on its 400 mile journey to the metropolis.  This station no longer exists.

Glasgow folk participated in their first railway experience in September 1831, when the Garnkirk and Glasgow Railway opened from Townhead. It was to be the only line until 1840, when the service to Ayr was introduced, followed by one to Greenock in 1841, and a service to our eastern capital of Edinburgh in 1842. London was linked via Carstairs and Carlisle in 1848. Many years later and much to the delight of small boys (and big ones too), there was sometimes the opportunity to watch rail crews indulging in unofficial racing. This was usually possible, for example, when the Kilmarnock and East Kilbride trains were both scheduled to depart St Enoch Station at 5.33 p.m. On 13 August 1965, when this picture was taken, the victor was the Killie train, ex LMS class 5 4-6-0 no. 44707, which drew ahead of its rival, BR standard 2-6-4T no. 80120, on the approach to Gorbals Junction where their paths diverged. On the closure of St Enoch station the following year, this junction was removed.

This was the steamy scene at Mount Florida station on 26 October 1955 when the 3.30 p.m. from Glasgow Central on the Cathcart Outer Circle line was hauled by British Railways standard 2-6-4 tank 80027. This type of locomotive is probably remembered fondly by many who owned the Hornby Dublo model of BR no. 80054, which was part of the same family. Like so many other small stations of the period, Mount Florida was complete with its John Menzies newspaper kiosk when this photograph was taken.

Glasgow's large municipal tramway system naturally required the employment of a team of maintenance men and vehicles. Many of the repairs were completed during the night when traffic was at its quietest and work could proceed quickly. However, it was sometimes necessary for emergency work to be carried out during daylight hours, as in this view looking east along Glasgow Road, Clydebank in 1924. It shows three Tramway Department solid-tyred Albion tower wagons with their crews repairing the overhead electric wires, while schoolboy spectators gather on the left to offer advice. Virtually nothing remains of this scene now; the tramways disappeared in the early 1960s and both the Empire Cinema and St James's Church were demolished during the late 1970s clearance programme in Clydebank.

Bunnets, bowlers and Brylcreem boys barging aboard busy cars specially provided for the football crowds leaving Ibrox Park after a Rangers match in the early 1930s. The second tram shows the destination James Street Bridge. This was an unusual short working which ran along Ballater Street and terminated on the Gorbals side of the Clyde at Glasgow Green. The reason for this was the closure of the bridge for reconstruction work between 1930 and 1933, during which time tramcars had to turn either side. The name L. MacKinnon on the side of the tram refers to Lachlan MacKinnon who was general manager of the Tramways Department at this time.

Glasgow's well-loved tramcars are still spoken about fondly by those who remember them – and also by many who don't! The first route, operated with horse-drawn trams by the privately-owned Glasgow Tramway & Omnibus Company, was opened in August 1872 from St George's Cross to Eglinton Toll. The municipal Glasgow Corporation Tramways Department took full control of the system from July 1894 and introduced their first electric cars in October 1898 between Springburn and Mitchell Street in the city centre. This was a quiet moment at Glasgow Cross in the summer of 1961. The clock on the Tron steeple shows 9.18 and tram 1162 is about to return along Trongate to Maryhill, having arrived at the Cross on a short working, rather than heading out to the zoo as was usual for most service 29 cars. The still familiar advert for Scotland's other national drink tops the now demolished Glasgow Cross railway station building which served the low level line from Glasgow Central to Rutherglen.

'Coronation' car 1270 in London Road approaching Glasgow Cross on a dreich day in 1961. A punter races over the greasy granite setts in an attempt to catch the car as it slows towards the stop ahead. Coronation tramcars were so named because of their introduction into the Corporation fleet at the time of the Coronation of King George VI in 1937. Because of their comfort they were the most popular type of tram in the city and served Glasgow well during their quarter century of operation. This one is seen on service 9 heading to Dalmuir West from Auchenshuggle, the last tram route to operate before eventual closure of the system in 1962.

A flower seller's cart can surely be permitted as coming under the title *Wheels Around Glasgow*. Taken on a fine summer day in 1960, one can almost imagine the scents and the colours, despite the monochrome illustration. This vendor had his stall opposite Lewis's store in Argyle Street. Another of the ubiquitous Coronation tramcars passes in the background.

A conductress steps out to board Corporation Standard car no. 126 on service 7, bound for Riddrie in May 1958, shortly before this route (which either connected Bellahouston with Riddrie, or went on further to Millerston) was withdrawn and replaced by trolleybus service 106 the following month. This photograph shows the trolley wires already in place for the impending conversion. The view looks up Cumbernauld Road from its junction with Duke Street. Paton Street, home to both the Dennistoun tram depot, which closed in November 1960, and to Beattie's bakery (now Rank Hovis), is just out of sight to the right. The Thornycroft van belonged to rival bakery, Bilsland's, of Hydepark Street, Anderston.

In addition to their electric tramcars, Glasgow Corporation also operated what by 1959 was the third largest fleet of trolleybuses in Britain. Often referred to as the 'silent death' after a number of fatalities involving these extremely quiet vehicles, their popularity in the city was muted, although they were very efficient and allowed a high passenger carrying capacity. Seen here in St Vincent Place in the mid-1950s are two examples on cross-city service 105, which connected Queen's Cross with the southern suburb of Clarkston. The trolleybuses were introduced to Glasgow in 1949, but were withdrawn after only 18 years in 1967.

Two of the then new trolleybuses passing the Tolbooth steeple at Glasgow Cross in the early 1950s. TB 5 (FYS 705) faces towards Saltmarket *en route* for Shawfield on service 101 while TB 21 (FYS 721) heads up the High Street to its terminus at Cathedral Street. The 'TB' fleet letters did not, as most Glaswegians naturally assumed, refer simply to trolleybus. 'T' stood for trolleybus while the 'B' meant that the chassis was built by British United Traction Ltd. Bodywork on these 6-wheelers was by Metro-Cammell of Birmingham, who not only built many of the city motorbuses and trolleybuses, but were also to construct the new subway coaches for the updated underground system in later years.

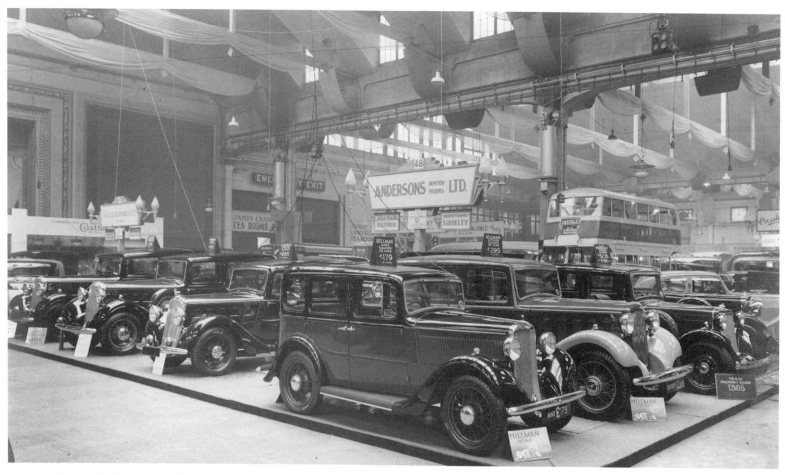

A motor show at the Kelvin Hall during the mid-1930s, with the display of Andersons Garage of Newton Mearns prominent. Andersons had established a business in Mearns village as early as 1832 and in their early years were coal merchants and contractors. Later they dealt in bicycles and by the turn of the century they were handling the pioneer motor cars. They became main agents for Armstrong Siddeley, Hillman and Humber cars and continued as Rootes Group dealers until their closure in 1980. The Mearns Cross shopping complex now covers part of the site of their former premises. This photo shows a Hillman Minx saloon priced at £179 and next to it a Hillman Sixteen saloon de luxe at £295. Next is an Armstrong Siddeley Twelve saloon, priced £305. Also visible is a Crossley double deck bus, while signs at the rear indicate that catering at the venue was provided by James Craig's luncheon and tea-rooms of Glasgow.

Glaswegians are extremely fortunate in having one of the world's finest transport museums, now housed in the Kelvin Hall, in their city. The official opening, performed by HM Queen Elizabeth, the Queen Mother, took place on Tuesday April 14, 1964 at the museum's previous location on the south-side, in what had been the Corporation Transport tramcar workshops in Albert Drive, Coplawhill. It is appropriate, therefore, that one of the main features of the collection was, and still is, a splendid selection of Glasgow 'caurs', ranging from a horse-drawn example to the still modern-looking Coronation and Cunarder types which were in operation until trams were withdrawn in 1962. Full-size Scottish railway locomotives and motor cars are also on display, and this view shows some of the latter, including Argyll, Beardmore and Arrol-Johnston at the original Coplawhill site alongside Standard car 1088 and single deck Duntocher car 1089.

Glasgow's clean and spacious Buchanan bus station, situated opposite the Concert Hall in Killermont Street, is one of the best in Britain. Things were not always thus, however. Initially there were no proper bus stations, but as services to and from the city began to mushroom from the mid-1920s onwards, provision had to be made for some form of regulated departure points. Street stances were provided in Carlton Place for destinations south of the Clyde, in Cathedral Street for destinations to the east and north-east, while Renfrew Street was used for those to the west and north-west (replaced later by covered bus stations at Waterloo Street and Killermont Street and an open bus station at Dundas Street). This 1936 view shows the stance along Clyde Street which replaced Carlton Place for south-western services. It was in use until Anderston bus station (now also closed) opened in 1971. Visible in this scene are Johnstone-bound Albion double and single deckers belonging to Youngs' Bus Service of Paisley, while Leyland double deckers owned by Central SMT and Western SMT may also be seen.

Maw, paw an' the weans hurry across the junction of St Vincent Street and Buchanan Street amongst the city traffic of 1935. I wonder if plus-fours will ever come back into fashion? Hopefully not! In the background a new Corporation Transport Albion Venturer bus heads up Buchanan Street past what is now the post office building on service 10A from Croftfoot to South Carntyne, passing a Morris Oxford Six fabric saloon of the early thirties. The bodywork on the double decker was constructed by Glasgow coachbuilders F. D. Cowieson & Co. of Charles Street, St Rollox, who built a large number of the Corporation buses in the pre-war years.

This view, looking northwards from St Enoch Square in the mid-1930s, illustrates just how congested Buchanan Street was even 60 years ago. In the foreground is an Armstrong Siddeley 12 saloon, while turning right from North Drive (a little-known Glasgow street which is now almost non-existent) is a Triumph Gloria. An Albion van owned by Bilsland's bakery and laden with bread baskets heads across the Argyle Street junction followed by a Western SMT bus bound for Newton Mearns. A line of Corporation buses drives up the street with Leyland Titan no. 219 at the rear showing Carntyne as its destination.

This view of Buchanan Street, taken at the junction with St Vincent Place, dates from 1936 and includes YS 5564, a brand new 8 hp Ford Y-type car built at the Dagenham factory, which opened in 1932. The two door model was Britain's first saloon car to be sold at only £100. The Corporation bus was a Leyland Titan with bodywork by Cowieson of St Rollox, operating on service 10 between Carntyne and Burnside, while the tram was heading for Dalmuir West on the green car service from Springfield Road.

Barr's Irn Bru is a household name throughout the country. The firm originated in Falkirk around 1830, cutting corks by hand to supply aerated water manufacturers, until Barr's commenced drinks production themselves in 1880. The Glasgow works opened in 1887 in Elba Lane, off what was then Great Eastern Road (now Gallowgate), adjacent to the Parkhead site where they remain today. This 1930s scene depicts a four in hand delivery wagon on James Street Bridge (officially King's Bridge), with Templeton's carpet factory visible beyond. This bridge across the Clyde connects Ballater Street with King's Drive, heading towards Bridgeton Cross. Barr's finally withdrew their horse-drawn delivery wagons in the late 1950s.

An example of one of Barr's early motor delivery vehicles, painted in the distinctive red livery still carried today. This was a 24 hp two ton Albion lorry of 1927 bodied in Greenock by McIntyre the coachbuilder. Note that the name of Barr's best known product (made in Scotland from girders) was spelt 'Iron Brew' at the time. Compelled by food agency regulations, the name was later shrewdly changed to 'Irn Bru' with the effect that the pronunciation remained the same but the meaning was changed to comply with the law's demands regarding description of the contents.

The Rankin Brothers were among the best known charabanc and motorbus proprietors of the 1920s in Glasgow. They had a city office at 58 Dundas Street, and depots in Muirhead, Balfron and East Kilbride. This scene shows one of their Rolls Royce charabancs about to depart from the Dundas Street office on a day excursion to the Trossachs. A board promotes an afternoon tour to Ayr and Burns' Country, while in the window extended tours to Whitley Bay, the Lake District, Blackpool and Scarborough are advertised. Rankin Brothers had several similar Rolls Royce charabancs which had originally been private cars but had their chassis lengthened by Mechans of Scotstoun and replacement 14 seat bodies built by Cadogan of Perth.

Two of the wee grey school buses, once a familiar sight around the city and sometimes referred to as ambulances, which were provided by Glasgow Corporation Education Authority for the transport of mentally and physically infirm children. This scene from the mid-1930s shows a group of children leaving for home after attendance at a 'special' school in Cathcart. The buses were both Albions, GD 8270 being a 24 hp model which had entered service in 1927. YS 3407 was a new Victor model of 1935 with bodywork by Wm. Park, coachbuilders, Kilbirnie Street.

'Mother, Here Comes the Castlebank Man' was the familiar slogan on the sides of the yellow Albion vans operated by the erstwhile Castlebank Laundry Company. This view shows a line of these delivery vans outside the laundry and dyeworks at Anniesland in the mid-1930s. Also known as the 'Franco Barbe Cleaners', the company was established in the nineteenth century and was one of Glasgow's oldest laundries, originally known as the Castlebank Steam Carpet Beating Works.

Bus queues such as this are now rarely seen. As increasing numbers of private cars appeared on our streets the lengths of the bus queues proportionately diminished. The swing to private motoring has gone too far, however, with our city streets choked with traffic and parking at a premium. This mid-1950s scene shows McNair Street in Shettleston, which was the terminal point for buses to and from the east end municipal housing developments at Queenslie, Ruchazie and Garthamlock. Lowland Motorways was based in Shettleston and one of their fleet of second-hand double deckers (this one had formerly served with Plymouth Corporation) reduces the queue somewhat. Lowland sold out to the predatory SMT company in 1958. The number of ladies wearing head squares is typical of that era.

# Albion 16-h.p. Delivery Van.

Load capacity 15 to 40 cwts., exclusive of weight of Body and Two Persons.     Chassis Specification, see page 12 of Catalogue.

Price of Van, complete, with Two Paraffin Head Lamps, Tail Lamp, Horn, and Tools.

|  |  | Length. | Breadth. | Height. |  |  |  | Code Word. |
|---|---|---|---|---|---|---|---|---|
| **15-cwt. Type,** Internal Dimensions, | - | - 6-ft. 0-in. | by 5-ft. 0-in. | by 5-ft. 3-in., | £432 | 0 | 0 | SONROSEOS. |
| **20-cwt. Type,** ,, ,, | - | - 7 ft. 0-in. | by 5-ft. 0-in. | by 5-ft. 6-in., | 443 | 0 | 0 | SONSACO. |
| **25-cwt. Type,** ,, ,, | - | - 8 ft. 3-in. | by 5-ft. 0-in. | by 5-ft. 6-in., | 475 | 0 | 0 | SONTUOSO. |
| **30-cwt. Type,** ,, ,, | - | - 9-ft. 6-in. | by 5-ft. 0-in. | by 5-ft. 6-in., | 522 | 0 | 0 | SOOTFLAKE. |
| **40-cwt. Type,** ,, ,, | - | - 10-ft. 9-in. | by 5-ft. 0-in. | by 5-ft. 6-in., | 532 | 0 | 0 | SONSHIP. |

Body Painted and Varnished, or Varnished only, to suit Customers' requirements.     Lettering extra.

Estimates and Drawings given for any type of Body.

A page from the 1908 Albion Motors sales brochure which pictures a 16 hp delivery van in service with Bayne and Duckett, Glasgow's well-known boot and shoemakers, still in existence today.  During those Edwardian days Albion Motors, whose factory was in South Street, Scotstoun, had a city showroom at 88 Mitchell Street.  In 1999 Albion celebrated its centenary year and while the firm is still in South Street, albeit at a different location, it no longer produces complete vehicles, specialising now in axles and other components.  Sadly, neither is it a Scottish company now, having been since late 1998 a wholly owned subsidiary of the US automotive systems organisation American Axle & Manufacturing Co. of Detroit.